Department of Education and Science

Information technology from 5 to 16

GW00702081

Curriculum Matters 15

AN HMI SERIES

LONDON · HER MAJESTY'S STATIONERY OFFICE

First published 1989
Second impression 1989

ISBN 0 11 270683 5

Contents

Preface

All the National Curriculum Subject Working Groups are being asked to indicate the potential for using information technology (IT) and developing capability in its use in their particular areas. In particular, the Design and Technology Curriculum Working Group has been asked to recommend attainment targets and programmes of study which provide a framework for the development of IT capability across a range of subject areas. In the light of reports from the Subject Working Groups and following consultation and the advice of the National Curriculum Council, attainment targets and programmes of study in the subjects, including some which relate to IT, will be written into Statutory Orders. Thus these attainment targets and programmes of study, particularly those related to Design and Technology, will provide the framework for the planning, delivery and assessment of work related to IT.

Since 1984 HM Inspectorate has published a number of Curriculum Matters papers designed to stimulate discussion about the curriculum as a whole and its component parts. *Information technology from 5 to 16*, the fifteenth in the series, sets out to help schools devise a coherent strategy for making effective use of IT, both in the enrichment of existing subjects and in learning about the technology itself. As such, its contents range more widely than the issues in the remit given to the Design and Technology Working Group. It focusses on the whole curriculum and addresses in some detail various aspects of learning which can be enhanced by IT. It discusses the implications for planning and management of IT in primary and secondary schools; the deployment of available resources; the assessment of pupils' work; and the place of computing as a specialist subject in secondary schools. This document seeks to build on national initiatives in this field. Insofar as it reflects the requirements spelt out in some of the Statutory Orders already published and practised in other areas of the curriculum, it identifies manageable elements of IT activities which can be developed by schools in the light of their particular circumstances. It is acknowledged that many schools do not yet have the hardware and software or expertise to enable them to pursue *all* the objectives proposed in this paper, but some of the objectives can be addressed in all schools having microcomputers and, as resources permit, this range of objectives can be broadened.

This document should be read as a whole, since all sections are interrelated.

Because of the forthcoming report from the Design and Technology Subject Working Group and the Secretary of State's subsequent proposals for attainment targets and programmes of study for IT, which will be subject to statutory consultation by the National Curriculum Council, we are not asking formally for responses to this discussion document. It is hoped that the issues it raises will enable teachers and others to respond to the statutory consultation.

Introduction

1. The twentieth century has seen an unparalleled rate of technological development leading to fundamental changes in our way of life and in the nature of society. Since the first powered flight in 1903 and the manufacture of the first microcomputer in Britain in the late 1970s, the speed of change has continued to increase. Latterly information technology (IT) has contributed significantly to these developments.

2. IT may be defined as the technology associated with the handling of information: its storage, processing and transmission in a variety of forms by electronic means, and its use in controlling the operation of machines and other devices.

3. IT is already a feature of everyday life. Many domestic appliances can now be programmed by means of microprocessors. Relatively inexpensive computerised toys, games and calculators are in common use. Supermarkets use bar code readers to list and price purchases and control stock. The recent growth in electronic communications enables teletext information to be obtained from the comfort of an armchair. Automatic cash dispensers check the details of an account and hand over money at times when the banks or building societies are closed. The world of work has been transformed by such devices as robots and word processors.

4. The national economy, international finance and employment patterns are profoundly affected by IT. This has led to fundamental changes in the way we do things at home and at work and in the range of facilities and artefacts available to us. In particular, today's citizen needs to be aware of the ways in which computerised information may be used, or abused.

5. Adults are still coming to terms with IT. Children take it for granted. Indeed, technology seems to give rise to great interest, and often excitement and pleasure, among young people. New technology has radically changed the home and the workplace: it has a similar potential to transform the classroom.

Aims of IT in schools

6. Children acquire the conventions and values of the new 'information age' from their experiences in and out of school and through the media. They learn about the capabilities, limitations and uses of computers, as well as of their associated technologies. Although IT is only one of a host of important factors affecting society and schools today, it is unusual among current agencies of change in that it impinges directly on the learner at all ages; on the nature and content of study; and therefore on the curriculum and the teacher.

7. IT has a critical role in enhancing the learning process at all levels and across a broad range of activities including but going beyond the National Curriculum. Through the use of IT in the curriculum, schools will also be helping pupils become knowledgeable about the nature of information, comfortable with the new technology and able to exploit its potential. The aims of working with IT in schools are:

i.   to enrich and extend learning throughout the curriculum, using the technology to support collaborative working, independent study and re-working of initial ideas as well as to enable pupils to work at a more demanding level by obviating some routine tasks;

ii. to help young people acquire confidence and pleasure in using IT, become familiar with some everyday applications and be able to evaluate the technology's potential and limitations;

iii. to encourage the flexibility and openness of mind necessary to adjust to, and take advantage of, the ever-quickening pace of technological change, while being alert to the ethical implications and consequences for individuals and society;

iv. to harness the power of the technology to help pupils with special educational needs or physical handicaps to increase their independence and develop their interests and abilities;

v.   to help interested pupils to undertake detailed study of computing and to design IT systems for solving problems.

Objectives for IT 5–16

8. All pupils should use a range of IT resources in core, other foundation and, where relevant, non-foundation subjects and cross-curricular themes. In the four key stages such resources might include electronic toys, calculators and musical instruments, as well as word processors and other computer software. The examples given within the following objectives are for illustration only. Opportunities for using IT within the classroom are many and technological change continues to add to and change them. Some of the objectives themselves may need review within a short span of time.

9. The differences in the backgrounds of pupils, their interests and the level of IT provision to which they have access outside school mean that confidence and skills in using IT are not related solely to the ages of pupils. Schools must build on whatever skills pupils bring with them and give individuals opportunities to share their knowledge with others and to employ such IT as is available in school and outside to further their learning.

10. During their time at school pupils' experience with IT should enable them to acquire certain knowledge, skills and understanding. Through work required within the National Curriculum and also related to other areas they should develop the general capability:

i.   to communicate ideas and information in a variety of forms using IT where appropriate (e.g. using word processing, electronic mail or desk-top publishing);

ii. to capture, store, gain access to, change and interpret information (e.g. using databases, spreadsheets or viewdata systems);

iii. to assess critically the content and presentation of information from various sources, including that in various databases (e.g. using viewdata or examples of computer-generated unsolicited personalised mail).

In addition they should be able:

iv. to carry out mathematical investigations or explore computer-based representations of imaginary situations or of real processes (e.g. using a simulation of an archaeological exploration or power supply network, or studying an economic model);

v. to make appropriate use of an IT system in the aesthetic activities of drawing, designing and making or composing (e.g. using an electronic music synthesiser, graphics software or a lathe controlled by a computer);

vi. to measure and control environmental variables and movement, using IT as appropriate alongside other resources (e.g. building an automatic device to count the number of times people enter a room);

vii. to consider and discuss some of the social changes and ethical considerations implicit in some uses of IT (e.g. databases containing financial information about individuals).

11. As they progress through the four key stages engaging in activities related to the above objectives pupils should acquire growing confidence and satisfaction in using IT and sensitivity to the wider implications of its use. They should develop a broad understanding of the ways in which particular systems work; familiarity with concepts associated with hardware and software; a vocabulary of terms associated with IT; and the capacity to learn from simply worded instructions how to operate unfamiliar technological devices. These aspects should be addressed within the context of mainstream curricular activities rather than in isolation.

12. The objectives are expanded on pages 9–32 to indicate the detail and depth of study appropriate to pupils in primary schools (key stages 1 and 2) and secondary schools (key stages 3 and 4). Some older secondary pupils, stimulated by their experience with IT, may wish to study a wide range of more advanced applications of computing. The last section deals with specific objectives for those pupils following specialist courses in computing or IT.

The general implications of IT for learning and teaching

13. Working with IT can motivate, excite and give pleasure to pupils of all ages. Both boys and girls often achieve levels of expertise with IT that surprise their teachers and themselves. There is value in allowing competence with IT to grow in the context of pleasurable learning. Such competence should be developed through activities which might be creative, investigative or involve games of strategy and tactics. These can provide fun and satisfaction while serving useful purposes.

14. It is important that schools identify the IT experiences pupils encounter outside school and seek to extend them. In primary schools boys and girls handle IT equipment with similar confidence. For various reasons, the interest boys have in technical artefacts is frequently reinforced during the late primary years and adolescence, whereas that of girls often lacks encouragement. Primary and secondary schools need to ensure that tasks set with IT systems match the level of expertise and interest of all pupils. Opportunities may need to be provided to compensate for limited experience of the technology.

15. IT is especially valuable in enabling pupils to take charge of their own learning and to work at their own pace. In particular, pupils with learning difficulties find stimulation through enjoyable repetition, coupled with a gradual increase in level of challenge. Extension work can sometimes be provided for more-able pupils using computer software. Pupils at any level who show specific aptitude and interest in IT must be encouraged to move ahead by exploring applications, and, for instance, writing software or designing hardware. This may occur individually or in groups, whether in class or in extra-curricular clubs.

16. Some approaches to work with IT can promote perseverance and self-esteem. If, after a series of tries, a pupil, or a group of pupils, fails to complete a task they will often re-define or subdivide the problem to bring it within the bounds of what is achievable. Moreover, no loss of face is involved in this process. Errors, wild approximations and apparent

malfunctions cease to be threatening indications of failure. Instead, they become inevitable, amusing, annoying and often fruitful stages in the process of creating, designing or finding a solution. Dissatisfaction with a written paragraph, musical composition, logic circuit or graphical design becomes a challenge to refine or improve. On some occasions, successive stages of development can and should be retained in order to allow review and to emphasise the value of the process as well as the final product.

17. IT has had a significant impact on the quality of presentation of pupils' work. It enables all pupils, including those with difficulties of physical co-ordination, to produce neat and accurate work and to concentrate on the quality of the content. This use of IT does not detract from the importance of handwriting as a component of the National Curriculum.

18. Although learning to use IT commonly involves practical work, it does not mean that tasks should constantly involve pupils in handling equipment. Much useful work takes place away from the hardware. For instance, in a simulation of pioneers crossing the American West, important processes will include research from facsimiles of original source materials, maps, artefacts and books; the exercise of imagination through discussions or role play about the lives of both settlers and indigenous people; and the formulation of collaborative decisions.

19. It is important for teachers to recognise that IT is only one of a range of sources of information but one with particular qualities. These include the speed of retrieval, the vastness of some databases and the facility to provide continuously updated material. A class project on life in the local community 100 years ago could make use of a database of census returns. Similarly a group of pupils producing a newspaper could have access to minute-by-minute reports from news agencies via a telecommunications link. Both examples would require pupils to decide which information was relevant to their tasks and to be discriminating in their choice of source. Census data stored on computer has the advantage of easing retrieval, but it is also important for pupils to be able to scrutinise facsimiles of original documents.

20. IT facilitates individual work, as when programs respond to a pupil's actions, and group work where, for example, there is a sense of shared ownership of a piece of collaborative writing on a screen. In such approaches, teachers become more than purveyors of knowledge or assessors of pupils' performance. They need, in particular, to be able to enter into the thinking of a group working on a task, in order to monitor and promote progress. This can be challenging because some uses of IT obscure the traces of pupils' thought processes as they work towards a solution or a finished product. Discussion may be needed to reveal insights or areas of difficulty and pupils should sometimes be encouraged to record interim stages of their work.

21. Increasingly, specially adapted IT systems offer an unprecedented degree of individual access to the curriculum for pupils with severe visual or physical impairment. Blind pupils could use a work station with Braille input and output, synthetic speech and text transcription facilities. Pupils with little or no hand control might use a computer through specialised switches. Large print displays or adapted keyboards can support pupils with less severe difficulties.

22. In the main, pupils should not regard IT and information-related activities as a distinct area of study whose principles and concepts need to be formally studied by all potential users. Most will find the technology easy to use. In schools the territory of IT should be the curriculum as a whole because it is there that its range of applications can be more fully exemplified and practised.

23. The nature and balance of much work within the curriculum are likely to be radically changed by the features described above. Compared with current practice there is likely to be increasing emphasis on the quality of communication; and greater stress on high-level thinking, on interpretation and on creative expression. Especially in the later key stages, the use of technology to measure, to collate and to display the results of experiments or investigations allows increased time for, and emphasis on, analysis and interpretation. More is then likely to be expected of pupils in terms of creative expression and conceptual understanding because of the reduced need to engage in or master routine techniques.

7

24.   Teachers are increasingly making use of IT for their own professional purposes and for the organisation and planning of the curriculum, for school management and for pupil assessment. Word processing and desk-top publishing encourage the production and regular revision of high-quality worksheets, schemes of work and school reports. Such use of IT will probably increase in the foreseeable future. The manifest use of computers in the management of a school increases pupils' awareness of IT. As their confidence grows, teachers may increasingly offer useful models to pupils.

IT in the primary curriculum

25. Young children readily accept IT; this is reflected in the way they assimilate new computer techniques. Whereas many adults may be hesitant and afraid of damaging an unfamiliar electronic device, children often attack it with uninhibited gusto. If particular keys do not have the desired effect, others will be tried. Even reception class infants can surprise their teachers by their adeptness in loading and accessing programs before being taught explicitly how to do so. Having watched others, they want to try – and frequently succeed – by themselves. It is important that children's capacities are recognised and encouraged throughout the primary age range, and that teachers are prepared to share their pupils' enthusiasm and to learn with them.

26. **To provide experience of sufficient depth, primary schools must inevitably be selective in their choice of IT activities although some elements will be mandatory in key stages 1 and 2 of the National Curriculum. In general, however, the knowledge and skills individual children acquire will necessarily vary from school to school, often depending on the extent of hardware available and on staff expertise.** Some applications (control technology for instance) require prior technical knowledge before they can be successfully introduced. During their primary years all pupils should develop confidence in the applications of IT identified by the school. The range of IT experiences needs to be widened progressively so that they support each of the objectives listed on pages 9–18.

Objective (i): Communicating ideas and information

27. Text handling using word processors can significantly improve both the quality and quantity of children's writing. Very young children with limited vocabulary can generate substantial pieces of writing by 'touching in' whole words

using an overlay keyboard. This facility can also support children with learning difficulties. The ease with which text can be drafted encourages more extended composition than does use of paper and pencil. Knowing that text may be easily manipulated encourages children to put their initial ideas into words. Older pupils may find it helpful to use the technology in order to plan and organise their ideas in visual and written form directly on the screen.

28.   Writing with pencil and paper is an essential skill and an important aspect of the National Curriculum. The teaching of handwriting should be complemented by giving children experience of text handling using word processors so that they can concentrate their attention on content and style. Redrafting (formerly an unwelcome, slow and messy chore) can be transformed into an easy, pleasurable and purposeful activity. The clear presentation of a child's work on a screen enables it to be read by groups of pupils and so opens up opportunities for sharing ideas about how a particular piece of writing can be improved. The lively debate that can ensue in the process of refinement of the text is as valuable, in learning terms, as the end product.

29.   When children have much that they want to write, lack of keyboard skills can be a serious handicap. It not only causes them to work at a painfully slow pace and thereby prevent others from using the hardware, but also frustrates those whose thinking races ahead of their ability to generate text on screen. In these circumstances a systematic approach to the acquisition of keyboard familiarity is necessary: children should undertake brief, structured practice using a suitable software package immediately before they start on a major writing task. The skill needed requires neither fingering technique, nor touch typing. It is necessary only insofar as it encourages children effectively to capture ideas as text in a form suitable for subsequent review and amendment. Such practice must not be tackled in isolation or become an end in itself.

30.   Pupils quickly appreciate the advantages of being able to use a simple computer thesaurus and to print text in various typefaces; of considering the role and layout of illustrations; of editing or using 'cut and paste' facilities; and adapting the style of presentation to meet different needs and readers. Not

all work need be destined for print: electronic mail and teletext format enable the children to present their writing to a variety of audiences. The desire to achieve high standards of content and presentation for such purposes may lead to collaborative working. This should fully involve pupils of all abilities and interests, whatever their level of skill in handling IT.

Related objectives

31. Through using IT as a medium for communicating information and ideas, pupils should, by the end of the primary years:

a. understand the ways in which a word processor can help in planning and undertaking a writing task;

b. be sufficiently familiar and adept with the standard keyboard to enable them effectively to translate ideas into text, and to produce a piece of work using such editing facilities as insertion, deletion and movement of text;

c. be able to rework their writing showing a sensitive awareness of readership, purpose and potential of the medium;

d. understand that the choice and order of words and illustrations, the format and size of text and graphics affect readability and impact.

Objectives (ii) and (iii): Information handling

32. Collecting, sorting and interpreting information are common practices with children of all abilities throughout the primary age range. For instance, infant children often gather data on their favourite colours or pets and then display this in pictorial or graphical form. The manual sorting of information on cards previously compiled by the children in an interesting context can serve to demonstrate how data can be structured and accessed. Subsequently, technology can extend the scope of such activities. For example, data collected on a particular

11

occasion can easily be compared with that obtained previously. The speed of operation of database or spreadsheet software enables more time to be devoted to the interpretation of results.

33. Children might start with an empty database containing a small number of previously prepared headings under which they enter their own data and begin to make simple comparisons. As they gain in experience and confidence more advanced techniques will be required. For instance, pupils will need to realise that if certain relationships are to be identified thought must be given to the headings under which information is stored and to the framing of questions by which it is to be interrogated. Older juniors might collect data about birds under different headings, such as physical characteristics, eating habits, habitats and predators. This information could subsequently be recorded on a computer database for display, discussion, analysis and interpretation.

34. IT facilitates the presentation of information in various forms, including graphical and tabular displays. Judicious choice of types of display can reveal interesting patterns of information. The excitement of discovering an obscure fact or unexpected quirk in a general pattern of information leads to children forming hypotheses to explain them. These can then be checked – and if necessary reformulated – by using reference books or source material. Typically, much of this work takes place away from the hardware and involves a high level of collaboration, research and discussion. However, the ability to access national or international databases through a telecommunications link can add exciting new dimensions to such work.

35. It is important from the outset that children adopt a critical attitude to the plausibility of displayed information. They also need to realise that a simple error in entering data can invalidate the results of an entire database or spreadsheet investigation.

Related objectives
36. Through handling and displaying information with IT where appropriate, pupils should by the end of the primary years:

a. know that computer-based information may exist in different forms (text, numbers, graphics);

b. be able to extract and display information in different ways from data previously stored by themselves or by others;

c. understand the need to question the reliability of displayed information and the fact that results produced by a computer may be influenced by the incorrect entry of data;

d. be able to interpret processed data and examine its plausibility;

e. be able to design a simple structure within which a limited set of data may be captured, stored and retrieved;

f. be able to interrogate data to examine patterns and relationships in the information and to form and test simple hypotheses.

Objective (iv): IT representations of real or imaginary situations and mathematical calculations

37. First-hand experience and educational visits are valuable ways of promoting learning but are not always feasible as some situations are too dangerous and some processes are too complex or expensive for pupils to witness. In these circumstances judiciously chosen computer simulations and adventures may be used instead. Pupils can encounter the unknown through journeys of discovery which introduce historical or mythical characters, locations, events and concepts. For young pupils, and some children with special educational needs, computer simulations can be a source of stimulus for language development. They also provide rich opportunities for collaboration in making decisions, examining ethical considerations, forming strategies and

solving problems. The capacity to retrace steps in a process, the ability to learn from mistakes and the development of social skills are valuable outcomes. So too is the unexpected revelation of qualities of organisation and leadership among members of groups working on simulations. However, judgement needs to be exercised over the relative quality of experiences offered by different media. A story can sometimes offer more than an adventure game and a film or television programme more than a simulation.

38. Computational skills are an important requirement of the attainment targets and programmes of study for mathematics. Such skills need to be practised. Access to an electronic calculator or computer can prevent children spending time unnecessarily on routine computation where this could obscure their understanding of underlying patterns and relationships. Typically, results of mathematical investigations undertaken in the classroom can be extrapolated to a degree or with an ease not otherwise feasible. Similarly, hypotheses can be speedily checked for their reasonableness and accuracy.

Related objectives
39. Through the use of computer-based adventures or simulations pupils should, by the end of the primary years:

a. understand that a computer may simulate a situation by following a set of rules consistently, although sometimes random elements may be incorporated;

b. understand that computer simulations are not complete and accurate representations of reality;

c. understand that a computer is able to act on a sequence of instructions from a user and that such a sequence may be stored;

d. be able to participate effectively in collaborative decision-making, whether as leader or team member;

e. be able to recognise when the use of an electronic calculator or computer is appropriate to the mathematical task in hand and be able to handle it competently.

Objective (v): The aesthetic aspect of the curriculum

40. Drawing, painting, modelling, performing, composing and listening provide exemplars of activities that contribute to the aesthetic and creative development of young children. Elements of visual imagery and sound are increasingly produced electronically. Children need opportunities to explore these through the use of IT, alongside more familiar and longer-established media.

41. Technology can be used to initiate and extend ideas in a variety of visual forms as well as to modify them. For example, images can be filled, rotated, overlaid or moved around the screen to develop pupils' visual perception, stimulate the imagination or to identify a range of possible designs. An image can be easily copied to produce a repeating pattern and the perspective of a three-dimensional shape can be altered almost instantaneously. The integration of text and images can transform an animated strip into an illustrated story, in which the visual elements and the time dimension in the presentation assume proper importance. Pupils' experiences can be further extended by using IT to investigate and capture a wider range of sounds than was previously possible. These sounds can be used alongside more traditional instruments to build confidence in exploring an exciting musical world. Programs, and hardware such as keyboards, synthesisers and other devices for capturing and modifying sound, can be used to enable children of all abilities either through group or individual activity to improvise, perform and experiment with both visual and musical ideas and to devise sustained compositions. Improvisations can be captured and compositions can be changed or edited to enable children to explore varying rhythms, structures, modes, tempi or sound colours. The continuing development of sensitive listening skills is an important feature of all these activities, which can be further extended by being harnessed to enhance other artistic endeavours such as dance or drama.

Related objectives
42. By exploiting IT in order to develop creative and aesthetic aspects of the curriculum, children should by the end of the primary years:

a. be able to create and store pieces of visual imagery and/or sound compositions;

b. be able to access and re-work existing sounds or images to produce controlled results which express their ideas;

c. be able to use IT sensitively in relation to different viewers or audiences.

Objective (vi): Designing, making, measuring and controlling in the physical environment

43. Primary children have an insatiable curiosity about the world and their immediate physical environment. They are interested in why events happen, what objects can do and how devices operate. Later, designing and making three-dimensional models or artefacts, especially when using resistant materials, enables them to appreciate the quality of man-made objects. The best of this work challenges pupils to solve real problems in areas of visual communication, product design and environmental control. This involves pupils in identification of the problem, recognition of different points of view (e.g. the designer, the user and those involved with production), exploration and realisation of ideas and evaluation. IT adds the exciting dimension of control by computer. In the early years, programmable toys and floor turtles enable children to initiate and observe movements of a remote object. This will involve estimation, measurement and comparison of actual and intended outcomes. Concepts of movement, length, angle of turn and relative position can be introduced. The actions of the device can be influenced by the use of simple programming commands, possibly presented on an overlay keyboard for very young pupils or those with learning difficulties. By devising a program of instructions to effect a particular sequence of movements the pupils are teaching the computer an algorithm for executing a task: in essence, infants are applying the principles of industrial robotics.

44. These processes require children to formulate their ideas and involve them in learning to refine their understanding of the problem until the desired outcome is achieved. An

extension of model-making and design activities is the use of interfaces. For instance, in connection with a topic on animals children could design a device that records the number of visits of birds to a feeding-table. The device might be triggered by micro switches, light beams or pressure pads. Besides skills of designing and making, such projects require the application of knowledge and skills gained from scientific, mathematical and environmental work. As well as mastering the technical operation of control systems, children should have their attention drawn to the need for quality in other aspects of the design process, particularly the aesthetic dimension.

Related objectives

45. Working with various tools, materials, sensors, switches and computers in science, mathematics, art and design, technology and environmental studies, children should by the end of the primary years:

a. understand from personal experience that certain toys, switches, domestic appliances and computers can respond to given signals or commands;

b. understand that a computer can control devices by means of a series of commands, and appreciate the need for precision in the framing of such commands;

c. know from personal experience that environmental changes can be detected, measured and responded to, particularly in domestic appliances or scientific measurements;

d. be able to construct a working model which responds only to certain environmental conditions;

e. be able to build a set of commands (a procedure) to control the movement of a screen image or a robot in an effective manner.

Objective (vii): Some consequences of IT for society and the individual

46. Throughout their years in the primary school, there will be many occasions when the children's work covers aspects of life on which IT exercises a significant influence. Some will be obvious. For instance, a visit to the supermarket in connection with a topic on 'Food' could include the impact of bar coding on stock control or on the format and readability of shopping bills. Use of IT in some libraries can enable children to discover book titles of interest to them which may be on the shelves at other libraries. They might be made aware of some types of data stored on computers, about books, about themselves as borrowers and about their recent borrowings.

47. Other changes may not be immediately apparent to children. A survey of the local community is unlikely to reveal the changing work practices brought about by the introduction of robotics in manufacturing industry. Similarly, children using electronic communications may not appreciate the distances messages travel or the large audiences they can reach, unless their attention is drawn to such facets. It is important, within such contexts, for children to consider the impact of the new technology.

Related objectives
48. Through visits in the community, general reading and the discussion of news items, pupils should by the end of the primary years:

a. know about everyday jobs which make use of IT;

b. know about types of information of interest to themselves and their families which may be held on computers;

c. be able to identify particular effects that a new or different IT application has had on themselves, their families or the community;

d. understand that technological developments have both advantages and disadvantages.

School policy

49. Although the 'new technology' has been generally available to primary schools only in the last few years, already computers have established their value in the primary classroom. The objectives discussed above offer a general guide for the directions in which schools might develop over the next few years. To achieve these objectives a clear school policy for realising the potential of IT across the curriculum is essential.

50. A starting-point could be to evaluate the type and extent of current use against the criteria outlined on pages 9–18. For instance, none of the four objectives in paragraph 31 would be met if the children were using a word processing package only to obtain printed copies of previously handwritten compositions corrected by the teacher. If such an evaluation revealed that while a broad range of work in IT had been covered much of it was superficial, a concentration on specific applications might be necessary to provide due rigour.

51. Modification of existing classroom practice could have significant implications for a school's deployment of hardware. A rota, for example, whereby IT resources are regularly allocated to certain classes for portions of a week, might not facilitate the depth of experience required: a system of negotiation by which particular classes retain the equipment for an extended period might be better. In that case care would be needed to ensure that no class suffered disadvantage over the school year. Alternatively, it might be decided to concentrate the use of all the school's IT equipment in certain classes or year groups.

52. The IT experience enjoyed by individual children within the school's chosen applications needs to be monitored and passed on to the secondary school. The development of confidence and competence for all the pupils involves far more than ensuring that each has access to the hardware on a similar number of occasions. Records should be maintained of individual progress and attainment along the principles described on pages 34–36. This need not be an onerous or time-consuming task, particularly if the technology itself is employed for the purpose.

53.   Reference to the potential of IT to enhance the various aspects of the children's work should be made throughout the school's curricular documentation, and reviewed regularly. IT objectives should be included. Supplementary materials, such as descriptions of suitable tasks involving IT with notes concerning commonly occurring technical problems, can be of considerable assistance to teachers.

54.   **Whatever the school's existing IT provision, realistic targets and a calendar for development need to be set. In determining which additional IT activities can successfully be incorporated into the work of the school, and at what stage, the issues of staff development and resource priorities will need to be considered.** Because of the expertise many teachers have acquired through working with computers in their classrooms, many schools are more self-sufficient in IT matters than they realise. However, the introduction of a wider range of applications requires a prior programme of professional development, which, because of the nature of a developing technology, will require regular updating.

55.   Involvement and commitment on the part of the headteacher are critical to the development of IT, but often the day-to-day leadership in this field is devolved to a member of the staff. Once an agreed plan of action has been adopted, however, every teacher – not just the head or 'IT expert' – should contribute to its implementation and periodic review.

IT in the secondary curriculum

56. Secondary schools need to identify what pupils from different primary schools have learned so as to complement and build upon their previous IT experiences. Learning across the curriculum should continue to be enriched through IT. The use of IT should sharpen judgement, improve skills and increase rigour and understanding of the technology itself. Such work is appropriate to pupils of all abilities.

57. IT in the secondary curriculum does not presuppose any particular form of organisation. Some schools are already moving towards the teaching of IT through different subjects of the curriculum rather than as a separate study. Others have chosen to provide specific computer awareness courses, mainly for pupils aged 11–13, a strategy which can be effective when courses are differentiated, fairly brief and especially when designed to build on pupils' experience of IT in the primary school. This may allow the teacher of English, for example, to assume that pupils have already been taught something about the elements of word processing. It is arguable, however, that these skills would be better developed from application within the programme of work in English. Many secondary schools operate a mixture of the two approaches.

Objective (i): Communicating ideas and information

58. The benefits of text handling packages in giving confidence to reluctant writers and allowing neat presentation regardless of physical co-ordination are just as applicable at the secondary stage as at the primary. Pupils increasingly appreciate the advantages of being able to enter text in different sizes, add paragraphs, 'cut', 'paste' and organise layout to accommodate illustrations. Use of a variety of fonts may become relevant at this stage, and it is important to consider the quality of visual impact of the final product. School news sheets and anthologies of pupils' writing have

proved excellent vehicles for composition and design as well as for group discussion. Where 'real' news is gathered, perhaps from a national agency through a modem, the selection of items as well as their editing and display becomes an issue for discussion. Sometimes this has to take place against deadlines imposed by a publication schedule. Care is needed in group work of this kind to ensure that all pupils are properly involved.

59. The redrafting of a pupil's unaided work on a computer is still uncommon in secondary schools, often because equipment is not readily available or suitably located. Where there are facilities, which might include programs to check spelling or offer synonyms, they may be used in a variety of ways. Sometimes successive drafts might have to be produced quickly as new information comes to light while on other occasions it is desirable to concentrate on the process of change in a document and the reasons for changes. The purpose of reviewing written work should be to consider tone and style, to refine description and perhaps to evaluate the work from the point of view of a variety of readers, as well as to correct spelling and sentence construction. As ever, extensive and varied reading helps understanding of these features. With the proliferation of forms of communication, it is useful to consider both their appropriateness for different purposes and the formality of language, for instance, which are suitable to them. Many of the foregoing considerations could be applied within the context of modern language teaching, where the ability to redraft writing and prepare foreign language news sheets has proved stimulating to children.

60. Access to word processors may offer valuable support and greatly increased motivation to pupils with special educational needs.

Related objectives
61. Many of the technical skills for handling text needed in the secondary school may well have been acquired at the primary stage. Progression here should be pursued in terms of more demanding writing tasks across a wide range of curriculum contexts rather than through the introduction of increasingly sophisticated word processing techniques. By the age of 16, all pupils should be able:

a. to understand the power of text handling packages to help organise and refine writing in terms of style and elegance of language, appropriateness or accuracy;

b. to select an appropriate IT application to create and communicate spoken or written text;

c. to exercise judgement in selecting and refining material in response to changing circumstances or new information, using IT where appropriate;

d. to use an IT system to compose a page of text which is easy to read and has visual impact.

Objective (ii): Information handling

62. Pupils will continue to collect, organise and analyse data but they should begin to take more responsibility for its validity and accuracy. They should also be encouraged to decide the appropriateness of various methods for handling data. For example, a spreadsheet might be used to carry out analyses of the nutritional value of meals being prepared in home economics and a database to record observed characteristics of insects found by a local pond. When gathering the data and using it to answer questions, test hypotheses or simply add to the database, pupils should learn to assess the accuracy of the data being used and its suitability for various analyses. Larger amounts of data, for example on the weather, may be aggregated over a period of time and compared with the data collected on another occasion, perhaps by a different class.

63. The skills of sorting, displaying and interpreting information are important throughout the years of schooling and should be practised along with other approaches to detect patterns and to present conclusions. It is important that the computer database does not replace first-hand use of documents, data, specimens or artefacts. The computer should be used to allow pupils more time to interpret patterns of data and results from investigations and to gain confidence in summarising information in various ways, including

graphical and tabular forms. The handling of census data using spreadsheet or database software, for example, does not always require extensive use of the keyboard; a large part of the work will take place away from the machine and will frequently involve discussion in groups. Similarly, the most valuable aspect of the experience of devising a teletext database of employment opportunities in the school's neighbourhood is the classification and organisation on paper of a system of menus and routes through which the intended user may gain access to the information rather than detailed design of individual screens.

Related objectives
64. By the age of 16 pupils should be able:

a.   to retrieve previously stored information in order to detect patterns and to form and test increasingly sophisticated hypotheses;

b.   to recognise circumstances in which IT offers an appropriate solution to a problem in data handling;

c.   to understand that techniques of enquiry may fail to reveal full information;

d.   to design a structure by which a set of data may be captured, stored and retrieved.

Objective (iii): Accuracy and validity of information

65. Work in IT should provide opportunities for pupils to learn that inaccurate data or too loosely constructed expressions in a questionnaire can lead to unexpected results. Above all, the gathering of large volumes of data should alert pupils to the need for care in assessing accuracy and reliability. Measurements derived from IT devices should be subjected to commonsense scientific and mathematical checks and viewed alongside data obtained by previously conventional means.

Related objectives

66. By the age of 16 pupils should be able:

a. to recognise unexpected or odd results;

b. to employ regularly commonsense methods to check the validity of data;

c. to understand that an enquiry can only be as successful as its source material is accurately and consistently gathered.

Objective (iv): Simulation and modelling

67. Older pupils may explore computer simulations of real environments, such as the ecology of an island. They may investigate the effect on local ecology of changing environmental factors in the island, such as the enclosure of land for grazing or its development for mining or industry. Within their geographical studies pupils may discuss population growth by using the UN's demographic data. In studying economic awareness they could manipulate factors which affect the running of a company. Similarly it is possible to study the effects of gravity and propulsion on the trajectory of a rocket and observe and calculate parameters governing radioactive decay. In this way processes can be studied which would not be accessible to pupils for a variety of reasons, such as the time scale of an observation, cost or the danger of actual measurement.

68. There are aspects of the curriculum concerned with designing and making where simulations can mirror industrial practice to avoid the waste of time and valuable materials or components. For example, complex calculations involved in designing a beam to carry specific loads may be carried out by a computer program or the action of a computer-controlled lathe simulated on a screen before committing the cutting tool to metal.

69. It is important that a simulation is not accepted as a true representation of reality. The existence of an underlying

mathematical basis and its nature should be discussed as far as this is comprehensible to pupils. The use of simulations rarely means that pupils need to spend a lot of time working at computers. It is important to have time and space to think about the implications of particular simulation runs and to interpret at particular stages the information obtained from them, such as summary statistics or results in a business game. Pupils should also have opportunities to construct their own computer models of situations and to refine and investigate them. For example, they may construct a model of a tuck-shop budget using a spreadsheet in order to forecast profits and stock purchases given different pricing policies. They may explore the behaviour of mathematical functions they encounter by studying the characteristics of their graphs on a calculator or computer display.

70. While it is not envisaged that all pupils would undertake the detailed study of a programming language they should understand the concept of a computer program as a set of instructions. This understanding can be promoted by the use of certain drawing or control packages where a sequence of moves can be 'saved up' and executed together. The contribution of particular instructions to the whole can be examined without discussing in detail the underlying algorithm. Some pupils will have acquired a detailed knowledge of programming by using computers at home or by specialist study at school. It is important to take account of what will be a much greater divergence in attainment than is often found in other areas of the curriculum so as not to frustrate interested pupils.

71. Many of these aspects of IT will affect mathematics. Using elementary principles of programming pupils can, with perhaps only a few lines of coding, tackle a mathematical problem or investigation, perhaps using probability theory to model a real event such as the forming of queues at a petrol station. Mathematical tools which carry out certain functions (graph plotters, spreadsheets, statistics packages, interpreters of algebraic expressions, etc.) are available for the microcomputers used in schools, offices and homes. Moreover some of these functions are becoming available on mass-produced calculators. Pupils need to be confident and sensible in handling numbers, formulae and numerical relationships mentally so that they are sufficiently competent to turn to IT

only when necessary, but then to use it effectively. Those manipulations and skills which are essential to the development of sound mathematical concepts and fluency in applying them will continue to need strengthening but there is little sense, for instance, in spending many weeks teaching fluency with routine techniques for solving particular equations when solutions can be obtained by pressing a few keys on a calculator. Instead, the time is needed for the development of other skills and knowledge, such as how to investigate and detect mathematical relationships and draw conclusions from them; how to let IT tools represent statistical information; how to check that results obtained using IT are sensible; and how to formulate a problem in ways which allow the use of IT in the solution.

Related objectives

72. As a result of using simulations and modelling in a number of subject areas, by the age of 16 pupils should be able:

a. to understand that dangerous or costly investigations, or those not easily measured because of long or short time spans, can be simulated by using IT;

b. to understand that a computer procedure or program is a set of instructions to be followed in a pre-determined sequence;

c. to understand that simulations rely on underlying mathematical models and procedures, devised by a designer, which can only approximate to reality;

d. to use suitable software to implement a computer model;

e. to change the data and the rules governing a simple computer model and explain the effects;

f. to select appropriate instructions or rules and procedures to model given situations;

g. to carry out a mathematical investigation using IT, particularly where the calculations would be unwieldy otherwise.

Objective (v): The aesthetic aspect of the curriculum

73. Within creative, design and artistic activities a computer can be particularly effective in both the exploratory and refining stages. It complements established and more familiar media.

74. In understanding the characteristics of effective communication, pupils should appreciate the match between presentation, content and the needs of a target audience. To this end practical activities might, for example, involve enquiries into the communication implications of variation of typeface styles, sizes and weights, alternative juxtapositions of text and illustrations within page layouts, and the opportunities presented by 'cut and paste' techniques.

75. In art and design, the computer can provide the opportunity to create images using a combination of traditional skills and such images can be captured, developed and manipulated using a variety of devices. Some physically handicapped students with difficulties of motor control find IT devices easier to manipulate than conventional media. IT can also provide the scope to explore the elements associated with the development, analysis and evaluation of visual imagery such as line, colour, pattern, texture, shape and form by copying, moving, changing, filling and combining areas on the screen without having to repeat sometimes tedious processes. The ability to recall and refine drawings, using computer-aided drawing and design (CAD) packages combined with the facility to translate two-dimensional views into three-dimensional representations, are powerful tools for working out ideas which may subsequently be realised in such resistant materials as wood, metal, plastic or textiles.

76. The use of IT can enhance and extend the range of pupils' experiences in music. It enables them to explore new sounds; to create, develop, refine and record their musical ideas and improvisations irrespective of their previously learned instrumental skills. Pupils may work together or individually on a variety of musical tasks; some using synthesisers and sequencers to compose their music, building up the strands part by part while exploring such aspects as texture and form; others may play their pieces to one another for immediate

critical appraisal and subsequent refinement. Adding improvisations on traditional instruments to electronic compositions can enhance the music and increase musical demands made of the pupils. The selective use of headphones can instil confidence because initial efforts are audible only to the pupils involved and their teacher, and recent developments with touch screens are making the musical potential of the computer more accessible to all, including those with special educational needs. The role of the teacher as sensitive consultant and classroom manager is crucial in these circumstances, where, of necessity, different musical activities may be going on simultaneously in various teaching spaces.

Related objectives
77. As a result of a wide variety of experience in a number of curricular areas, but particularly in creative and artistic activities, by the age of 16 pupils should be able:

a. to draw, model, design and compose or improvise using IT and refine as necessary;

b. to understand the value of IT to the creative process in providing a bank of images or sounds from which it is possible to select and which can be altered;

c. to explore two- and three-dimensional images, using IT as an aid to visualising and making an artefact;

d. to use IT to concentrate their listening in order to form creative judgements about their music.

Objective (vi): Measuring and controlling
78. Developing insights gained in primary schools, pupils may use interfaces for work in technology. This may be an extension of model-making and design. It could involve not only the programming of more complex sequences of controlled movements but also reacting to changing circumstances. For instance, the pressure exerted by a small animal on the floor of its cage as it approaches its trough, the presence of moisture in the trough, the intensity of light and

the ambient temperature could all be detected and used to trigger a microelectronic circuit supplying a given quantity of feed or switching on a heater.

79. Such experiences of control bring together knowledge and skills from a variety of subjects, particularly mathematics, science and technology. Used alongside conventional techniques of measurement and recording, IT can allow pupils to take rapid, accurate and multiple readings of physical and environmental quantities and of rapid processes. The temperature of a pond may be measured over several days or the voltage across a capacitor measured 100 times in one tenth of a second. Such measurements can yield more accurate and rapid results than some conventional methods, and can encourage pupils to assess the quality of data and refine experimental technique. Pupils' understanding of the dynamic nature of such phenomena as weather patterns and plant growth would also be improved. Similarly, direct measurement of the position of a trolley on a slope or of an object on an air track allows calculation and display of velocity and acceleration as they take place. Pupils with visual impairment, who find conventional techniques of measurement inaccessible, may be helped by devices using large-scale visual displays or synthetic speech.

Related objectives
80.   By the age of 16 pupils should be able:

a.   to understand that devices can be made to respond to data from sensors, distinguishing analogue from digital signals;

b.   to understand that experimental results can be obtained over long or short periods of time or at a distance using data-logging equipment;

c.   to set up simple experiments using IT to sense environmental variables;

d.   to construct a simple device which responds to data from sensors;

e.   to invent a procedure to control the movement of a device.

Objective (vii): Some consequences of IT for society and the individual

81. Pupils should be encouraged to identify and discuss applications of IT in which the accuracy of information about individuals is particularly important, for instance when creating and using a database containing personal information. They might discuss the social and economic consequences of IT such as the effect on the nature and pattern of employment; electronic surveillance; and access to, security and possible misuse of personal information stored on computers. Discussion of these topics is perhaps best undertaken in the context of humanities or personal and social education and of practical activities. For instance, a greater understanding of the changing nature of office work, and IT links enabling people to work from home, is more likely to come about when the topics arise incidentally within a practical word processing session than if discussed in isolation. As well as those jobs which have become more demanding as a result of the incorporation of IT, mention should be made of the effects of de-skilling on some craftsmen.

82. Pupils should also be made aware of some of the ethical implications of too easy access to personal information on computer databases. The impact of IT on such issues as the ownership of confidential information or the easy reproduction of copyright material might be explored within personal and social education or religious education. Similarly, the opportunities IT affords to pupils or others to produce newspapers or information sheets and reach relatively wide audiences raises pertinent issues of the selection of news items and balanced reporting.

Related objectives
83. By the age of 16 pupils should:

a. know about a range of jobs, the nature of which has changed as a result of IT;

b. understand that electronically stored personal information is easier to misuse than that kept in conventional form;

c. know about some effects of inaccurate data on files relating to personal information;

31

d. understand the implications of access to such information by various people or organisations;

e. be able to identify potential benefits and disadvantages for individuals, groups or society brought about by the introduction of IT.

Issues for school management

84. The learning objectives discussed above offer a general guide for the directions in which schools might develop over the next few years. The shift of emphasis towards the integration of IT into the curriculum as a whole places demands on both the management and teaching force of secondary schools. These demands relate to the formulation of a school strategy, curriculum design, provision and deployment of resources, and staff support.

85. It is part of the role of senior and middle management to review the use of IT regularly so as to ensure that sensible, planned experiences in IT are available to all pupils, and not only those taking certain subject options or taught by particular teachers. Curriculum planning should also take account of the need to arrange appropriately demanding IT work for pupils of varying levels of ability, interest and experience, including those whose IT skills are still insecure.

86. The identification of IT's potential contribution to the work of a wide range of subjects is clearly essential in ensuring better co-ordinated experiences for pupils. Discussions about this and the contribution of individual departments to the school's overall IT objectives must involve heads of department and subject staff. The drawing-up of detailed schemes of work setting out the place of IT in various areas of the curriculum is more likely to lead to a change of practice for the better if individual departments identify with the plans.

87. The distribution of resources within the school influences classroom practice in IT. There are occasions when a room is needed with enough equipment to occupy a whole

class, perhaps with two or three pupils working together at each micro. On other occasions teachers will need the use of just two or three micros located in their normal teaching bases as additional resources – the monitoring of scientific experiments and the use of a nutrition database during the preparation of meals in home economics are obvious examples. In addition some teachers will feel more at ease bringing IT equipment into their usual teaching room rather than moving to what they perceive to be a high-technology environment. Flexible arrangements are needed to meet individual teachers' circumstances. The balance of use between specialist computing or IT courses and the mainstream curriculum is a matter for senior management to consider since it very often entails a departure from established practice and a conflict of needs which are individually justifiable. The school library should be regarded as a natural place for IT alongside other information and learning resources.

88.   Suitable in-service training is crucial to success in an area like IT, which evolves so rapidly. While some teachers regularly exploit the potential of IT in their subject many lack the necessary confidence and expertise. There is a need for basic familiarisation with IT, but this is best provided in the context of a common classroom application. Regular updating is needed for teachers who are already confident in the use of IT and, in particular, for those with responsibility for specialist teaching in IT or computing. The pressing need for more training in applications of IT should not, however, obscure the need for guidance, preferably provided by teachers whose background is in the subject concerned, in good general classroom practice involving the use of IT.

89.   Some schools have set up working parties to address the issues discussed above. Such working parties are most successful when they represent a wide cross-section of departments within the school, make use of the expertise of a teacher with designated responsibility for IT across the curriculum and have the guidance and support of a member of the senior management team. The latter should have oversight of all aspects of resources for learning, including IT and the library. The support of a technician can increase staff confidence in the use of IT.

Assessment and progression

90. Pupils' individual interests, their experience of IT outside school and the emphasis placed on different aspects of IT by particular primary schools mean that performance levels are likely to vary greatly. For instance, a pupil who has attended a primary school where information handling is a prominent feature of the work might achieve high levels of performance in that field but not in applications of control.

91. Assessment in IT as in other fields is inseparable from the teaching process and should build upon good classroom practice. The major purpose of assessment is to give information about the achievement of pupils so that teachers can arrange progressively demanding tasks or, as the report of the National Curriculum Task Group on Assessment and Testing (TGAT–1988) indicates, obtain a 'well articulated picture of the individual child's current strengths and future needs'.

92. Progression in this context means not that pupils necessarily use more sophisticated IT tools but that they apply such techniques as they have mastered to progressively more difficult problems through their curricular studies, or use them to extend themselves in their work in terms of quality, quantity or both.

93. Published schemes designed solely to assess technical competence in operating the equipment may motivate some pupils but have little educational value. They may also lead to impoverished classroom activities by focussing teachers' and pupils' attention on technical aspects alone. A test which aims only to reveal whether children are able to copy and erase files on a particular computer system would not be a good indicator of their ability to apply this knowledge in practical contexts, either at work or in school. These simplistic procedures could mislead parents, teachers and the pupils themselves.

94. Everyday classroom activities provide the most effective setting for reliable evaluation of pupils' use of IT, and the professional judgement of teachers must continue to be the foundation of assessment. Observation of children applying IT within their work across a range of subjects reveals the extent to which they have assimilated the technology's

potential to advance, enrich or enhance their performance. For example, the use of a computer to analyse and display data about the types of organism found on a seashore might well have raised the level of a pupil's understanding of this study beyond that which would otherwise have been expected. Such insight cannot be achieved by testing a narrow range of IT skills in isolation.

95. The objectives set out on pages 9–32 should be addressed, as far as possible, through various tasks designed to assess knowledge, skills and understanding across a range of curricular areas, as described in the TGAT report. Due credit should then be given for the attainment of these IT objectives, as well as for those relevant to other aspects of the curriculum. For example, a class of older children might be given the task of developing and concluding a story after listening to its opening episodes. In assessing the piece of work attention will be paid to linguistic and literary features such as the quality of the vocabulary, the sequencing of events, sensitivity to readership and the richness of characterisation. Some children may have used a word processor to undertake this work. This will give the teacher an opportunity to assess the pupils' IT skills by observing their competence in such aspects as using the technology in planning their key ideas, in transferring their thoughts to the screen with appropriate speed and in refining their initial efforts. This redrafting may involve replacing words with synonyms after using a computer thesaurus or moving blocks of text. A secondary science class may be asked to design experiments to investigate the effect of environmental factors on the rate of growth of plants in a greenhouse. Pupils' competence in setting up equipment and using software to obtain readings and graphical representations of these results would be assessed as a measure of their attainment of IT objectives. The choice of appropriate variables to measure, the placing of sensors and the time intervals chosen in order to test a clearly stated hypothesis would give some indication of their understanding of the scientific principles involved.

96. Assessment of pupils' competence to use IT by the teacher of another subject will take time to become established. Until schools and teachers have become familiar with a variety of applications of IT, testing of some aspects of IT capability may have to take place separately, albeit within

the context of tasks that have meaning for the individual learner.

97.   Assessment by the pupil of his or her own achievement is often an intrinsic part of learning. Children are often more critical of themselves than an observing adult would be, particularly in the case of IT. They are inclined to accept the response of the technology to their own instructions as a fair, impartial and unthreatening indicator of the quality of their work. Moreover, as pupils become familiar with a particular IT package or artefact their expectations of it, and consequently of themselves, often rise appreciably.

Computing as a specialist subject

Aims of computing as a specialist study

98. The secondary curriculum should also cater for the needs of those pupils with a special interest in studying information systems and computer applications in greater depth. Computing as a specialist subject now has to build on pupils' cumulative experience of IT within the school and elsewhere, as described in previous sections. The aim of computing as a specialist study should be to extend, unify and deepen pupils' understanding of computer technology and its applications. In particular computing should help pupils:

- to study the capabilities and limitations of a broad range of applications and the contexts in which they are useful;

- to analyse systems and to apply IT creatively in the solution of problems using reasoning, judgement and persistence;

- to study ways in which computer applications affect the operation and management of industrial and commercial concerns or public services;

- to gain some understanding of the working of systems which extend users' mental and physical functions and capabilities;

- to carry out sustained pieces of work that *are* formally assessed related to the application of computer technology in society.

Objectives of computing

99. The pace of technological change, and pupils' growing familiarity with IT, mean that objectives in computing need to be reviewed at frequent intervals. Pupils specialising in computing should have acquired the facility with IT indicated in earlier sections. In addition, by the age of 16, they should be able:

- to make explicit the techniques used in arriving at solutions using computers. This is a fundamental objective and involves:

  i.   the formulation of a problem and determination of whether a computer solution would be appropriate;

  ii. the collection and management of data relevant to the solution of a problem;

  iii. the iterative processes of evaluation and refinement both of problem formulation and of solution;

  iv. subdivision, where necessary, of a problem into an organised collection of smaller problems;

  v.   the choice of appropriate software, equipment and methods to design and implement a solution to a problem;

  vi. the presentation of a solution together with appropriate documentation.

- to understand the context in which computers are used, and in particular:

  i.   be familiar with a broad range of contemporary computer applications, including those used in schools;

  ii. know the range of commercial and industrial contexts in which computers are used;

  iii. know about social effects that the aggregation of information in computer systems and its general accessibility may have;

  iv. be able to discriminate between good and poor user guides to computer applications.

- to understand the fundamentals of computer-based technology, i.e.:

    i.   understand the function of software and of hardware in a computer system (e.g. different levels of software, software controlling peripherals, firmware);

    ii. know how computers store, manipulate and transmit information;

    iii. know about a range of common computing machinery and the principal functions of devices that may be attached (e.g. devices for communication between mainframes and micros, or for processing remotely sensed data);

    iv. know the broad principles of how communications within and between computer systems work;

    v.   understand how to construct simple programs in a structured programming language.

Teaching and learning

100.   Solving problems is an activity which appears in most subject areas. Computing, however, offers a particularly rich supply of problems which can be dealt with at different levels and which can be solved in different ways. A solution, however effective, can almost always be improved, and it is often possible to suggest improvements to the way the problem was originally described. The problem may succumb to a wide range of solutions, from rapier thrust to sustained bludgeoning. For example, a street of houses may be drawn on a screen by means of the painstaking repetition of elementary commands in the LOGO language or more briefly and elegantly by calling a few previously built routines. Both types of solution need to be developed at various stages of learning, and students should be encouraged to generate their own problems.

101.   Even at the simplest level, the first answer to a problem rarely works as its author expects it to, so that the process of

exhaustively testing and correcting a solution is an integral part of the activity. More complex problems, such as those tackled in project work, require clear problem delineation, planning and subdivision into more manageable tasks.

102. Projects produced in computing are extremely varied, and at their best can contribute to the life of the community. For instance, a stock control system designed by a pupil for a small local factory may subsequently be used by its staff; hardware and software are often designed to help disabled persons; a database of local parish records may be compiled for use by the church; and systems could be devised to help with the administration of school sports fixtures and their teams. All these require the skills set out above as problem-solving objectives, and should involve pupils in many contacts outside the classroom. The project work done by the most-able students may be of an almost professional standard, which may raise the expectations of examiners and teachers to an unrealistically high level. It is clearly desirable to encourage work of such a standard, but it should not lead to the setting of performance levels that penalise the competent student.

103. Not all pupils will be interested in solving comp-utational problems by developing programs in a language like BASIC, LOGO or PASCAL or in assembly code. They may use applications software such as a spreadsheet to investigate possible methods of solution when solving realistic problems. Where programming is involved, a 'tool-box' approach has been found useful. It can enable students to complete and test complex programs without being subjected to the frustrations of having to produce accurate detailed coding. Such a 'tool-box' may be a set of accurately coded routines, or parts of programs, written by professional programmers. Each routine, or module, performs a specified task, such as displaying a pie-chart or checking whether data is numeric or alphabetic. The use of these pre-written routines allows pupils to construct whole systems by selecting and linking them without getting involved in too much detail. It is common to find that the modules do not satisfy their users for long and that pupils have to modify them as they refine their problem specification and improve their solution.

104. A computing class may undertake to provide a comprehensible guide to an application such as a computer-

aided learning package. In doing so they need to bear in mind the expectations and needs of different users of the package; for instance teachers and students, with and without some computing expertise, would form a useful forum for discussion of the need for and requirements of good documentation.

105.   The above activity lends itself well to differentiation of provision for pupils with various needs and interests. The levels of challenge and the areas of interest of any application being scrutinised should be matched as far as possible to the student group. In lessons involving an introduction to solving problems through programming, for example, all pupils, including those familiar with some aspects of programming, should have available a progression of problems of increasing challenge. For instance, two problems might be introduced, one involving the simple manipulation of characters on the screen and another involving arithmetic calculation. After class discussion of a handful of relevant programming commands some pupils might be helped by having versions of simple programs which go some way towards a solution. More experienced and knowledgeable pupils may be given related but harder programs, or some which contain omissions or even errors. Similar principles might apply in solving problems using spreadsheets, control technology or databases.

106.   It is particularly important that a variety of teaching and learning styles should be used in computing work. Much of the work should be practical, but it need not necessarily all be done at the computer. The teaching of all the objectives would be assisted by the use of directed reading, extended class discussion, note-taking by the students, simulation by the teacher of certain processes on a computer, class visits to computer installations, demonstration of computer concepts with the computers available, and the use of films and videos. Such a varied approach is still unusual; all too often the teaching is characterised by lecturing and dictated notes, many of which, however accurate, are not fully understood by the students.

107.   A great deal of the methodology of teaching computing evolved when computers were scarce – often there was only one slow terminal or micro in a class for a limited time. The content and style of teaching now need to be adapted to take

account of the access boys and girls have to increasingly sophisticated computers and information both inside and outside schools.

Assessment

108. The assessment of project work has always been a part of computing courses. This has developed from simply writing programs to the systematic description of a solution, perhaps, but not necessarily, involving programming. The assessment of this work has necessarily been carried out by teachers rather than by examination boards directly. The testing of problem-solving skills is attempted largely by project or extended course work whereas the knowledged-based objectives are mainly tested by written examinations. This is not necessarily the best approach. Extended problem-solving exercises based on a case study or design brief can be devised and are likely to be better indicators of pupils' capacities than many conventional projects.

109. Assessment of course work in computing poses a major question of how teachers and examiners might assess work produced co-operatively. Such co-operative work would mirror common and effective practice in the world outside of school. There is experience of assessing group projects within higher education, and the move to more assessment by teachers gives the flexibility that is needed if this is to be tried in schools.

Organisation

110. The number of pupils opting for examinable courses in computing is usually greater than the school can provide for. This is either because of a lack of equipment or, more commonly, of appropriately trained staff. Disappointed students become disenchanted, as do some who start computing courses but find their expectations unfulfilled. This situation can be avoided through counselling and offering pupils first-hand experience of IT in various subjects before options are chosen. Pupils specialising in computing should have access to computers in at least half of their lesson time,

with a ratio of about three pupils to two micros in these lessons. These lessons may be in special computer rooms or in classrooms close to shared computing facilities if supervision is satisfactory. Those lessons not taught in computer rooms need not necessarily concern themselves entirely with theory. Practical aspects of computing can be demonstrated using a single micro equipped with a large screen.

111. The ratio of boys to girls in computing classes is about 2 to 1, which is unsatisfactory. It is even greater in computer club activities, which are almost entirely confined to boys unless special arrangements are made to set aside time or computers for the exclusive use of girls. Since it is difficult to see what is intrinsically more appealing to boys than to girls in the nature of computing, considerable care, and often positive encouragement, are needed in counselling pupils about available courses. Computer clubs can be successful in attracting girls when activities are chosen which do not emphasise traditional male preoccupations with technicalities.

112. There is at present a number of courses entitled 'information technology' which are different in emphasis from 'computer studies'. In general, information technology courses are concerned less with how computers work and little about using a programming language. However, changes in emphasis in recent years have meant that both subjects are now more concerned with the application of computers. Nevertheless, there can be a divergence of interest and it may be that two courses will continue to develop. One may be a basic course in information technology with an emphasis on the practical use of database, text handling, spreadsheet and graphics packages and the other a more demanding computing course. The latter would place greater emphasis on the analysis and design of systems, an understanding of computers and their applications, and the production of software. Whatever pattern of courses evolves, the main concern will remain the improvement of the quality and range of educational activity in these various areas and an accent on understanding.

113. For this to happen there will need to be a proper consideration of curriculum development in computing, for the training and re-training of specialist teachers and for the provision of material resources. Firmer links will also be needed between computer users outside schools and teachers

involved in specialist work. Implementation of IT in the curriculum, in the ways suggested in the previous sections, can be significantly helped by the enthusiasm and expertise of pupils and staff engaged in specialist computer work. There is thus a need within each secondary school for pupils who, in addition to being competent in the day-to-day uses of IT in the general curriculum, also have a deeper understanding of microelectronics-based technologies and the processes involved in using them effectively. UK schools have achieved novel and interesting uses of IT in the general curriculum, and these have often resulted from co-operation between computing specialists and imaginative curriculum innovators.

Appendix

The work of curriculum subjects and its relationship to IT

A school needs to formulate a plan for the development of skills and attitudes related to IT through activities across the curriculum. One useful model of how IT concepts can be related to activities in various subject studies is shown below. Many of the skills and attitudes listed clearly overlap. This is intentional, and emphasises the major messages of IT for the learner within different contexts.

The curriculum should aim to develop pupils' understanding of IT through appropriate use in such contexts.

1. Art

a. Use computer-aided design (CAD) to develop, organise, evaluate and refine ideas in visual form.

b. Use IT to support existing art and design media, as well as to generate imagery.

c. Be able to select with discrimination from a range of input devices, such as a mouse, keyboard and digitiser, and to comprehend the basic capacity of a system to perform a particular task.

d. Use IT databases of materials, media, technical data, records and resources.

2. Craft, design and technology

a. Measure and control the physical environment using IT-based equipment.

b. Recognise and diagnose a problem in a control system and solve it, e.g. by modifying an existing computer program or piece of logic or communication circuitry.

c. Arrive at acceptable draughts using computer-aided design to generate a series of models.

d. Participate in group activities and discussion to select equipment, including microelectronics components and software most likely to facilitate a solution to a problem; and communicate justifiable proposals.

e. Use databases of, for instance, materials, parts and designs.

3. Geography

a. Measure phenomena in the environment (using directly or remotely sensed outputs).

b. Manipulate and explore such information and communicate conclusions.

c. Explore computer-based simulations of geographical phenomena.

4. History and social sciences

a. Access, retrieve, evaluate, interpret historical, political, social and economic information from various sources, including computer databases.

b. Structure, collect, code and store information to facilitate retrieval and communication.

c. Discuss issues arising from IT today, such as de-skilling, employment patterns, communications, in relation to other social/economic revolutions.

d. Explore historical concepts via computer simulations.

e. Discuss the impact of IT and information on data protection, the individual and society.

5. Home economics

a. Command a sufficient vocabulary of common terms to understand and discuss how to use everyday IT systems.

b. Learn from written, graphic or recorded-speech instructions how to operate an unfamiliar IT system (e.g. a radio alarm, a digital meter, a calculator, or a microcomputer program).

c. Sensibly measure and control activities with IT, e.g. time an oven.

d. Investigate computer-based representations of real situations, e.g. a home or meal plan.

e. Discuss how IT is used in everyday applications, e.g. bar codes, automatic banking machines, teletext in the home, and viewdata systems such as those used for holiday booking in travel agencies.

f. Use databases of, for instance, materials, goods and nutrient values.

g. Be aware that IT is a pervasive, powerful resource, but that one should not become too dependent on it or accept uncritically data processed with IT.

6. Language/English

a. Use IT to help in the generation and composition of both written (prose and verse) and spoken language.

b. Use IT to send and receive spoken and written messages.

c. Choose suitable language for the medium used.

d. Choose suitable language for that particular audience which is using the medium at that time.

e. As personal experience of c and d above is gained, develop a growing critical awareness in appraising choices made by language users in the context of IT.

7. Mathematics

a. Use sensibly numerical, algebraic, graphical and programmable calculators, and a spreadsheet facility; discover from documentation how to operate an unfamiliar calculator or micro.

b. Use sensibly rudiments of a simple programming language with graphics facilities; understand what a simple sequence on instructions within a specific computer application or in a computer language would cause the computer to do.

c. Solve problems involving detection of pattern or relationship with IT; utilise a variety of strategies, including iteration to a solution.

d. Construct and investigate computer-based represent-ations of mathematical situations.

e. Participate in group activities in respect of c and d above, and report orally.

8. Modern languages
a. Use various forms of text handling, from authoring programs, where input is controlled by the teacher, through free composition using word processors to desk-top publishing.

b. Use IT to communicate with remote partners in the UK and abroad, e.g. via the exchange of audio or video recordings, electronic mail or satellite programmes.

c. Explore programs such as computer simulations, interactive video and databases, which provide scope for discussion and decision-making.

9. Music
a. Use IT with discrimination to compose, manipulate, refine and produce music of quality.

b. Generate new sounds for creative development.

c. Explore musical patterns and contrapuntal devices.

10. Physical education
a. Determine and comment on physical fitness, using computers with suitable sensors to measure and analyse physical performance data, e.g. rates of heartbeat or breathing.

11. Religious education
a. Intelligently discuss consequences of IT for the indiv-idual and society.

b. Be aware of challenges to individual conscience in respect of misuse of information, ownership of ideas/software, invasion of privacy, computer crime.

12. Science

a. Measure and control scientific processes, using IT where appropriate.

b. Have a sufficient vocabulary of terms to discuss how to use everyday IT systems and how they communicate with their environment, including the user.

c. Understand the functions of common components of IT.

d. Explore computer-based simulations of processes.

e. Use computers to store and retrieve scientific data as appropriate.

Glossary/index of specialist terms

The numbers shown refer to pages.

Algorithm: a sequence of operations describing a solution to a problem in a finite number of steps. See also *Programming*

Analogue: an analogue measurement represents a quantity by displaying a continuous signal. For example a quantity of electricity used may be represented by the turning of a dial. See also *Data representation*

Animation: a sequence of images which are rapidly superimposed one on another to produce the impression of movement.

Application: the use of the *computer* to solve specific user tasks in the processing of *data*. An applications package is a set of specialised *programs* and associated documentation to carry out a particular application, such as the control of a company's stock.

Bar code: a pattern of lines of different thicknesses giving coded information about the item to which it relates, such as an ISBN book number.

BASIC: See *Computer language*

Calculator: a device designed to manipulate and display numerical data. Sophisticated electronic calculators can be *programmed* for specific applications and may be able to display results in a graphical form or as algebraic expressions.

CD-ROM: a device for storing large quantities of *data* using a compact disc similar to those used for recording music in a *digital* form. ROM stands for 'read only memory', i.e. the data stored is fixed and can be read, but not changed.

Central processing unit: the main part of the computer which processes instructions and controls the operation of the *computer system*. See also *Computer, Hardware*

Computer: an electrical machine which can both process and store *information*; the information may consist of numbers, words, symbols or images or any combination of these. A computer accepts information using an *input unit*. The information is processed by a *central processing unit* and the results are supplied by an *output unit*. A computer is controlled by means of instructions given in the form of a program.

Computer-aided drawing and design (CAD): the use of a computer in producing drawings and designs for industrial, engineering, aesthetic or scientific purposes. Drawings, produced on the screen, are stored in the computer and can be manipulated to produce a design in a variety of perspectives and with special effects. See also *Application, Computer*

Computer control: the use of a computer to control machinery or to monitor a given environment and respond appropriately to any changes which may occur. For example, if both the *input* and *output units* are connected to a manufacturing process, outputs from the process may be used as input to the computer, which can then be used to control the process.

Computer language: a defined set of characters and symbols which may be combined by specific rules to produce an artificial language for communicating instructions to *programmable* machines. See also *Programming*

Computer system: a *central processing unit* together with its *input* and *output* devices and any *software* required. See also *Computer, Hardware, Software*

Data: any group of facts, numbers or symbols which describe a state, a value or a condition. Data usually describes a fact or an event; it is contrasted with *information* which is conveyed by a set of data, and with a computer *program* which is a set of instructions operating on data.

data 6, 11-13, 18, 27, 31, 35, 38-40, 45-49
data capture 3, 10, 13, 15, 24, 28
data from *sensors* 30
data protection 46
remotely sensed data 39
validity 23-25

Data-logging: the use of a device to capture data and record it immediately so that the data may be processed at a later date.

data-logging equipment 30

Data representation: the way in which data is held and organised in a *computer*. The majority of computers represent data internally in *digital* form. Data from the environment, such as sound waves from a speaker, is often received in *analogue* form. For the computer to represent and respond to many real events, it is therefore necessary to be able to convert data from *analogue* to *digital* and vice versa.

Database: a collection of structured data where the structure of the data is independent of any particular application. Databases are created, updated and accessed by special *software* called a database management system.

Desk-top publishing: a computer applications package which facilitates the integration and production of text and graphics within a document. See also *Application*

Digital: a digital measurement represents a quantity, such as time, by displaying a discrete signal which changes by steps. In a digital computer, data is represented by combinations of discrete states usually symbolised by 0 and 1. See also *Calculator, Data representation*

Electronic mail: the sending of written messages, from one *computer* to another, by telephone. Messages are stored in a central *computer system* to be retrieved when the recipient subsequently communicates with the central computer by telephone. See also *Text handling*

Firmware: See *Software*

Floor turtles: an electro-mechanical device, controlled by LOGO or another *computer language*, for executing movements, drawing designs, and activating sound or light effects. See also *Programming*

Graphics: the representation of *information* by the computer in graphical form. The display may be as charts, diagrams, pictures or *animations*. Special devices are required to produce paper copies of graphical data.

graph plotters 26
graphics *software* 4

Hardware: the name given to the physical components of a *computer system*. It includes both the *logic circuit* and *logic gates* forming the *central processing unit* and other *peripheral* devices, such as keyboards, screens and printers, which are connected to it.

automatic device 1, 4, 46-47
computer-controlled lathe 25
computer system 34, 39
hardware 4-6, 9-10, 39-40
interface 17, 29
keyboard (including overlay) 10-11, 16, 24, 45
logic circuit 6,46
modem 22
mouse 48
peripherals 39
pressure pads 17
radio alarm 46
sensor 17, 30, 35, 48
synthesisers 4, 15, 28
telecommunications link 6, 12
touch screen 29

Information: a collection of items, such as text, *data*, symbols, images or sounds which conveys meaning.

information 1-4, 6-7, 11-13, 21-27, 31-34, 37-39, 42, 46-49
information systems 37
information technology 1, 43, 45

Information technology: the application of appropriate technologies to the processing of information. In general, this currently refers to the use of computing, telecommunications and digital electronics. See *Information and p.1*

Input unit: a device, such as a keyboard, that puts *data* or instructions into a computer. It allows people to communicate with computers and may accept either coded *information* or human readable information such as magnetic ink or optical characters. See also *Computer*

Interface: the hardware and associated software needed between *processors* and *peripheral* devices, to compensate for the differences in their operating characteristics. See also *Hardware*

Logic circuit: an electronic circuit made from a combination of *logic gates* to perform a particular logical operation.

Logic gate: an electronic switch which may have more than one input, but only one output. The output is activated when a given set of input conditions are met.

LOGO: See *Computer language*

Modem: a device capable of transforming computer data so that it may be transmitted or received via a telephone line or radio link.

Mouse: an input device which the user moves around a flat surface in order to select the required response from a *computer system*, e.g. to move a cursor around the screen.

Output unit: a device that receives *data* from a *central processor* which it either stores or outputs in human readable form, such as a printer or graph plotter. See also *Computer*

PASCAL: See *Computer language*

Peripheral: the term used to described input, output, or other devices which can be connected to a *central processing unit*.

Program: a set of instructions in a *computer language* for executing an *algorithm*.

Programmable item: any device that stores a sequence of instructions which are carried out automatically, such as a cooker, toy, or *calculator*. See also *Calculator, Software*

Programming: the process of producing a finite set of rules, or algorithm, giving a sequence of operations for solving a specific problem. The final step requires writing, or coding, the algorithm in a form which the computer can understand and the process includes testing to ensure that the results produced are correct.

> *algorithm* 16, 26
> assembly code 40
> *BASIC* language 40
> coding 18, 26, 40
> *computer language* 45
> computer *software* 3, 5
> interpreters 26
> *LOGO* language 39-40
> microcomputer *program* 46
> *PASCAL* language 40
> programmable toys and *floor turtles* 16
> tool-box 40

Remotely sensed data: data associated with *information*, such as the height of a river, which is collected by *sensors* positioned either on site or remotely and transmitted electronically. See also *Data*

Sensor: a device with an input which measures some external phenomenon quantitatively and an output which can be read by a *computer*, for example, a thermometer which produces a *digital* output. See also *Hardware*

Simulation: the use of a computer to process a model of a real or imaginary system. Simulations may be used to study the behaviour of systems which would be difficult, impossible or dangerous to reproduce in the classroom.

> adventure game 13-14
> computer models 26-27
> computer simulation 43
> simulations 4, 6, 13-14, 25-27, 41, 46-49

Software: the *programs,* routines, procedures and packages together with their associated documentation which can be implemented on a *computer system.* Some of the software may be permanently installed on 'read only memory' within the computer and this is known as firmware.

> *computer system* 34,39
> *firmware* 39

Spreadsheet: a computer applications package which allows the user to record, structure and manipulate numerical data easily. See also *Application*

Synthetic speech: the simulation of human speech by *hardware* and *software* within a *computer system.*

Teletext: a computer-based *information* retrieval system which uses screens of text and simple graphics. The information is displayed in pages and may be broadcast by television or via the telephone. *Viewdata* is the general term for interactive systems such as PRESTEL, where information may be transmitted as well as received.

> teletext 1, 24, 46
> teletext format 11
> teletext in the home 47
> viewdata systems 3, 47

Text handling: the processing to textual material. It includes the use of a *computer system* to assist with the tasks of editing and printing documents and the use of the telephone system to transmit data from one location to another.

> *electronic mail* 3, 11
> text handling 9, 21, 23, 43
> *word processing* 3, 8, 19, 22
> word processor 1, 3, 9-11, 22, 35

Thesaurus: a lexicon of words and phrases classified according to meaning or ideas. See also *Computer*

Touch screen: an input device which senses the position of a user's contact with the screen of a computer monitor. See also *Hardware*

Validity: the extent to which stored data is free of errors. Reliable computer systems perform checks in order to reduce the number of errors. See also *Data, Data representation*

Viewdata: See *Teletext*

Word processing: A computer applications package which can be used for creating, amending, formatting and printing text and tables. See also *Application, Text handling*